Longman English Tips Book

Elizabeth Cripps

LONGMAN
London and New York

Mariana PO

Addison Wesley Longman Limited
Edinburgh Gate, Harlow,
Essex CM20 2JE, England
and Associated Companies throughout the World.

0582 303 98–2
First Published 1997. Reprinted 1998

British Library Cataloguing-in-Publication Data
A catalogue record for this book is available from the British
Library

Set by 30 in 9/11 Baskerville
Produced by Addison Wesley Longman China Limited, Hong Kong
GCC/02

Contents

Introduction

Where should I put the apostrophe? Does that word begin with a 'c' or an 's'? Do you write 'I'm angry with' or 'I'm angry at' someone? Questions like these occur to us every day when we are writing. They may crop up when we are preparing for examinations or – even worse – when we are actually taking them. There are so many points to check, to make sure that they are correct, that sometimes we hardly know where to begin.

This *Longman English Tips Book* is designed to help you to find answers to some of these problems quickly, and also to help you to make the best use of your time, as you study and revise for your English examinations. The general reader should also find the accessible style of this book of great benefit.

Punctuation

Capitals

Use a capital letter for:

days of the week, months, public holidays

Sunday	January	December
Easter	Independence Day	Labour Day

languages, nations, religions

English	French	Catholicism
England	France	Judaism

personal names and titles

John	Mr. John Jones	Sergeant Bilko
Nadia	Dr. Nadia Ali	Prince Charles

places

Buckingham Palace	London	the United Kingdom
Pall Mall	England	Europe

titles of books and films

<u>Animal Farm</u>	<u>Anthology of</u>	<u>The Life of John F.</u>
<u>Reservoir Dogs</u>	<u>Ghost Stories</u>	<u>Kennedy</u>
	<u>Ghostbusters</u>	<u>J.F.K.</u>

*Also use a capital for personal pronoun **I**:*
How can I become rich and famous?

And . . . to begin a sentence:
The careers master asked me what I intended to do after leaving school, until I became rich and famous.

Commas

Use commas to separate parts of a sentence to help the reader to understand the meaning more easily:

before a conjunction

The man lay dying, but nobody called an ambulance.
They said April would be wet, but I have got a sun-tan.

after an adverbial phrase or clause

Because I could not wait, I left the party early.
While practising on the ski slope, she hurt her leg.

for parentheses (brackets)

Some people, as you know, are dreadful gossips.
Her dress, a pale shade of pink, looked gorgeous.

to separate contrasting phrases

Chess is a game of skill, not of chance.
You can either come with us, or stay at home.

to separate parts of a list

They packed shirts, sweaters, anoraks and walking boots for the school trip.
The first, second, third and fourth runners were all record breakers.

to introduce speech

The President said, 'Welcome, one and all!'
The Master of Ceremonies announced, 'The Right Honourable Herbert Wilson'.

before a tag* question

It is the right answer, isn't it?
You will come to the party, won't you?

* A tag turns a statement into a question.

Full Stops

Use full stops:

at the end of every sentence

First of all she won the county league award. Her next achievement was to succeed in the all-England championship. Finally, she gained a place in the Junior Olympics.

Also . . . after abbreviations and shortened words

Mr.   etc.   U.N.O.

Semi-colons and Colons

Use semi-colons:

for a slightly longer pause than a comma

Chess is a game of skill; bridge is a game of chance.
(Chess is a game of skill, not of chance.)

to separate the main parts of a long sentence

I had prepared carefully for the party with, firstly, plenty of
cans of lager and soft drinks; there were twenty different types
of sandwiches, white bread and wholemeal; lastly, I bought six
large cakes and cut them into portions – that should be
enough to feed everyone.

Use colons occasionally, but essentially to:

introduce a list

There are three pieces of advice for the learner driver: use
your mirror, don't drive too fast and be patient.
It was a genuine antique: the right wood, colour, style and
period.

introduce a comment or explanation

He never had much luck: he lost a contact lens while looking for a four-leaved clover.
The job is quite demanding: you must be prepared to be here from seven in the morning until eight in the evening.

Dashes and Hypens

Use dashes also occasionally, but essentially to:

separate a comment, or an aside, from the sentence

The new neighbours – from California I am told – moved in last week.

show a break in speech

Overcome by embarrassment, she started hesitantly: 'I'll try to – I mean I – I will keep this brief…'

pause before a climax

The instructor was counting for her jump: 'One, two, three – and she was air-borne.'

introduce or mark the end of a list

London, Paris, Rome – all these she visited.
One, two, three, four, then a silence – and I was flying.

Use hyphens to:

link compound words

double-parked   X-ray   cross-examine

divide a word (by syllable) at the end of a line

The school trip to Egypt was understand-
ably very popular.

Apostrophes

Use an apostrophe to show possession:
's for one person

Tony's photographs are spectacular.
A child's eye view of the world is refreshing.

s' for more than one person

The tourists' photographs are spectacular.
Reflectors in the road surface resemble cats' glinting eyes.

....

➤ NOTE

1. **In a sentence where more than one person is named as owning something, use 's after the last person's name.**
   Tina, Ryan and Peter's project was judged to be the best.

2. For words ending with an s put 's or s'.

The dress's fastening was jammed.

The dresses' colours were too bright.

3. For plurals without an s, use 's.

The women's chances were increased.

....

omission i.e. one or more letters have been missed out

I wouldn't like to go = I would not like to go.

It's time to leave   = It is time to leave.

....

➤ NOTE

No apostrophe for the following: its, his, hers, ours, yours, theirs as possessive adjectives or pronouns.

Its fur gets dirty when it's (i.e. it is) chasing rabbits.

They are ours, not yours, you know.

Apostrophes should not be used for plurals.

....

Underlining

Underline:

titles of books, journals, newspapers, films and plays

<u>Fear of Fat</u> is a best-selling paperback this year.

<u>The Times</u> is increasing its circulation.

<u>Gone With the Wind</u> is one of the world's best-known films.
<u>Cats</u> is touring in the United States at the moment.
(See also p. 11)

(See also p. 11)

➤ NOTE

Titles are normally italicised in printed books.

---

to emphasise occasional words or phrases

It <u>was</u> there when I looked last.

to indicate an unassimilated foreign word

It was a <u>zeitgeist</u>* film.

* The film fitted the mood of the times.

Numerals

Rule: *Spell out numbers that can be expressed in one or two words; use figures for others.*

twenty-five pounds	£2,259.60
twenty-two dollars	$2,221
five thousand voters	5,261 voters
ten million bushels	10,402,317 bushels
a thousand acres	672 acres

Rule: *Never use a number to begin a sentence.*
Two years ago, I went to Portugal for my summer holiday.

Rule: *Use numbers for addresses, book references, dates.*
My friend's flat was in a house at 22 St. Marks Road.
The article was in *Vogue*, vol. XXX, p. 15.
The letter was dated 6 May 1971.

➤ **NOTE**

If you have good reason to break the rules, be consistent in your use.
I was born on the sixth of May in the first year of the century.

Quotation Marks

Use quotations marks for:

a person's actual words

The Prime Minister rose: 'I bring to the attention of the House a matter of grave concern.'

a quotation from a book or other text

In the third act of the play, Hamlet reflects on the dilemma of facing up to his problems or taking his life: 'To be, or not to be – that is the question.'

titles of books, journals, films, plays (as alternative to underlining)

'Fear of Fat' is a best-selling paperback in the United States.

Punctuating Speech
Dialogue

Each speaker's name is followed by a colon. The speech is then set out, with each speaker taking a new line. Use normal punctuation, but no quotation marks.

Stranger: Where are all these people hurrying to?
Bystander: To catch the ferry over to the mainland.

Use square brackets to indicate stage setting, stage action.

[Scene 1. A narrow street, near the quay of a busy port. Two men stand on the pavement, watching.]
Stranger: where are all these people hurrying to?
Bystander: To catch the ferry over to the mainland.

Use curved brackets for brief comments about the speakers.

[Scene 1. A narrow street, near the quay of a busy port. Two men stand on the pavement, watching.]
Stranger: Where are all these people going?
Bystander: (irritably) to catch the ferry over to the mainland.

Direct Speech

Use double quotation marks for all the words of a speaker, even if they continue for several sentences.

"I'm afraid we have sold out of that title," said the assistant. "The new order should be here next week."

Change the full stop at the end of the sentence to a comma, before adding quotation marks and the verb. Question and exclamation marks, though, mark the end of the sentence, as usual.

"I'm afraid we have sold out of that title," said the assistant. "The new order should be here next week."
"But I need it now; I can't wait that long!" the customer exclaimed.
"Well," continued the assistant, * "why don't you try Bookworm, further up the High Street?"

> **NOTE**

1. **For each new speaker, start a new line.**
2. **Use a capital letter for the first word of the speech.**
*3. **If the sentence carries on after the speaker is named, do not use a capital letter again.**
4. **If you have speech within speech, use single quotation marks for the inner speech and double for that of the main speaker.**
   "You cheated! You clearly heard the umpire call 'Out!'"

As you see, punctuation is a matter of knowing the conventions of written English to pace your writing so that your reader may understand you more easily. It also has another – stylistic function – that is to create effects of calm, suspense or tension in the reader.

Effective Punctuation

Here is an example of a piece without punctuation: the character is lying in bed, with her mind freewheeling:

"I could always hear his voice talking when the room was crowded and watch him after that I pretended I was cool about him because he used to be a bit on the jealous side whenever he asked me who are you going to see and made me a present so that finished that I could quite easily get him to to made it up any time I know how…"

It works well here, doesn't it – but that is because it fits the stream of thoughts of the character.

Here are some paired examples to indicate some of the scope of stylistic punctuation. In each case A is the original punctuation; B is the punctuation after proof-reading.

A   He had the waiting crowd's attention. All was quiet. The diver removed the towel. He started walking to the diving board. Slowly he climbed the spiral stair tread by tread. He was ten metres above the pool. When he arrived at the top he stood still. He listened carefully. He could not hear a sound. He paced to the front edge of the board. He stood poised. He pressed downwards with all his strength. He lifted his arms. He launched upward and forward. Splash, in a fraction of a second it was all over, everyone was clapping and cheering. The judges announced the score, full marks the Gold medal.

B He had the waiting crowd's attention – all was quiet. The diver removed the towel. He started walking to the diving board; slowly, he climbed the spiral stair, tread by tread, until he was ten metres above the pool. When he arrived at the top, he stood still; he listened carefully but could not hear a sound. He paced to the front edge of the board, stood poised, pressed downwards with all his strength. He lifted his arms and launched upward and forward. Splash! In a fraction of a second it was all over. Everyone was clapping and cheering as the judges announced the score: full marks – the Gold medal!

➤ **NOTE**

Conjunctions have replaced some of the full stops, to give a smoother effect.

Here's another pair:

A The wind blows ever colder, ever fiercer. The sky never looked so black. She pulls her coat closer around her. It is quieter now as the wind dies a little. All she can hear are her own footsteps, clip clop clip clop clip clop. Suddenly there is a clap of thunder. A bolt of lightening blinds. Besides the clip clop she hears another sound. Is it the wind, could it possibly be what she fears? Surely it is not other footsteps. Someone is following steadily and quietly. Her footsteps quicken. She walks faster and faster just as those steps do behind her. Heart pounding and breath shortening she tries to speed up, she begins to run. By now she is frantic, she cries out help.

B   The wind blows ever colder, ever fiercer; the sky never looked so black. She pulls her coat closer around her. It is quieter now, as the wind dies a little. All she can hear are her own footsteps – clip clop, clip clop, clip clop. Suddenly, there is a clap of thunder; a bolt of lightning blinds. Besides the clip clop, she hears another sound. Is it the wind? Could it possibly be what she fears? Surely, it is not other footsteps? Someone is following, steadily and quietly. Her footsteps quicken. She walks faster and faster, just as those steps do behind her. Heart pounding and breath shortening, she tries to speed up; she begins to run. By now she is frantic; she cries out: "Help!"

Finally, here is a piece where the full effect of the ending depends on correct use of that minor punctuation mark – the dash. This is a version the student wrote first:

A [A girl has had an argument with her boy friend, during which he has dared her to take a bungee jump if she is proved wrong. It turns out that she *is* wrong. We take up the story from the point where she is preparing to jump.

... so it was agreed that on June 16th, at six o'clock in the morning, I was to go for the jump.

The spot chosen for the event was Vasterbron, an incredibly huge and majestic bridge connecting two small islands. There were five others going for a jump when we got there. If they were there for losing a bet or if they were truly insane is something I never found out. The instructors told us to decide on the order for who would jump first. I was to be second. Now I started to realise that this was reality and it made my heart pound and my blood rush through my veins. The first jumper went off, and made it back up again with liquid screams streaming from her mouth. My God I am going to die, I thought, as the instructor tied the straps around my ankles. A last look at Paul, I was silently begging please don't make me do this, but it was no use. He was standing there as if he was cut out of stone. I would get no mercy there. Well he was the one who would have to take care of the pieces and mourn for the rest of his life. I was the one who would die as a woman with her boots on. Ready. I'll count to three and on three you go. One, two, three, silence, and I was flying.

Now see how the repunctuated version brings out the drama, especially of the ending.

B The spot chosen for the event was Vasterbron, an incredibly huge and majestic bridge connecting two small islands. There were five others going for a jump when we got there. If they were there for losing a bet, or if they were truly insane is something I never found out! The instructors told us to decide on the order for who would jump first. I was to be second.

Now, I started to realise that this was reality; it made my heart pound and my blood rush through my veins. The first jumper went off, and made it back up again, with liquid screams streaming from her mouth. 'My God! I am going to die.' I thought, as the instructor tied the straps around my ankles. A last look at Paul. I was silently begging: 'Please, don't make me do this !' but it was no use. He was standing there as if he were cut out of stone. I would get no mercy there. Well, **he** was the one who would have to take care of the pieces and mourn for the rest of his life. **I** was the one who would die as a woman with her boots on.

"O.K. Ready? I'll count to three, and on *three* – you go. One … Two … **Three** …"

Silence – and I was flying.

Punctuation Exercises

Here are two passages which require punctuation to bring out the meaning effectively. Why not try them? You will find the correct versions on p. 81.

A

on the fourteenth of june nineteen ninety ernest threadfill a fifty nine year old accountant from gloucester thought to be involved in smuggling drugs placed thirty one thousand pounds in a bag in a rubbish bin at heathrow airport at one oclock in the afternoon the bag was collected by mister paul frost twenty five with nine children from a hundred and fourteen furze road in south london when he deposited what appeared to be a fast food box but which later was said to contain a number of packages of a substance thought to be heroin the british broadcasting corporation gave news coverage to this event at six oclock in the afternoon saying that both men had been detained for questioning mister frost later was reported to have said it was the hand of fate newspapers carried headlines to the effect that two master criminals had been outwitted by the police.

B

its the way he sits and waits vaguely watching the television vacantly staring out of the window it haunts me because hes just sitting and waiting he forgets my name my uncles names my cousins but he always remembers Brutus the dog he seems to know who I am but not why Im here I suppose Im here to pass by some of that long lonely waiting time with some light conversation Im here to prove that he has carried on his blood line maybe Im here to show its all been worth it four children ten grandchildren a fairly comfortable life but does that bring any solace when now his life is spent just sitting too weak to stand waiting.

Spelling

Most people have occasional problems with spelling and for some it can be a major difficulty. One reason is because English spelling is only partly to do with sounds: there are 26 letters to represent 40 different sounds.

Here are three approaches to help improve spelling:

Rules: recognize where letters are usually grouped together to represent the same or similar sounds;

Traps: recognize spellings where a letter or group of letters is silent;

Words that confuse: think positively about your own spelling difficulties and learn to lessen them by noticing and practising words that are easily confused.

Spelling Rules
1. *Pairs   –ie/–ei*

Rule: *i before e, except after c, if the sound is 'e'.*
–ie

achieve	niece
believe	piece
field	relieve

EXCEPTIONS! seize, counterfeit

–ei

conceive   perceive

deceive   receive

Rule: *Spelling may be either –ie or –ei, if the sound is not 'e'.*

–ie

efficient	lied	conscience	fiend
proficient	tied	patience	friend
sufficient	tried	science	

–ei

eight	weight	heir
height	foreign	their
neighbour	reign	leisure

2. Pairs   –ce/–cee

Rule: *After con–, inter–, re–, use –ce; otherwise use –cee.*

concede   precede

intercede   recede

Otherwise ...

exceed   proceed   succeed

3. Pairs −ce/−se

Rule: *Nouns are spelled with −ce.*

advice	licence
device	practice

Rule: *Verbs are spelled with −se.*

advise	license
devise	practise

4. Pairs −sion/−tion

Rule: *Words ending with the sound 'shun' are spelled −tion.*

administration	declaration	mention
attention	function	nation
collection	junction	prevention
exception	limitation	restriction

Rule: *Words ending with sound 'sheun' are spelled −sion.*

admission	expression	persuasion
collision	extension	session
decision	omission	succession
discussion	permission	transmission

5. Pairs   –el/–le

Rule: *Words ending with the sound 'el' are spelled –el.*

cancel	panel
channel	parcel
label	tassel
model	vowel

Rule: *Words ending with the sound 'ul' are spelled –le.*

angle	principle
bicycle	struggle
obstacle	vehicle

6. Pairs   –or/–ar

Rule: *Words indicating people's profession usually end –or.*

actor	governor	operator
author	instructor	sailor
conductor	mayor	solicitor
doctor	navigator	tailor

Otherwise ...

calendar	peculiar
cellar	popular

| familiar | regular |
| grammar | similar |

7. Pairs final e/– final e

Rule: *Words that end with the letter e lose the 'e' before a suffix beginning with a vowel.*

| acquiring | persuading |
| declaring | supposing |

Rule: *Words that end with the letter e keep the 'e' before a suffix that does not begin with a vowel.*

| advancement | likewise |
| basement | placement |

8. –ous

Rule: *When –ous is added to a word ending with –our, drop the letter 'u' in the spelling.*

amour	amorous
clamour	clamorous
glamour	glamorous
humour	humorous
odour	odorous
vigour	vigorous

9. –y

Rule: *When a word ends with consonant + y, change y to 'i' before adding a suffix.*

angry	angrier
busy	busier
early	earlier
easy	easier
deny	denied
try	tried

Rule: *When a word ends with a vowel + y, keep y before adding a suffix.*

buy	buyer
enjoy	enjoyment
pay	payer
play	player

10. Prefix and suffix joins

Rule: *Never add or subtract a letter at a join.*

Prefixes –

disappear	dis + appear
disappoint	dis + appoint
misapply	mis + apply
misspell	mis + spell
unnecessary	un + necessary
unnatural	un + natural

Suffixes –

fondness	fond + ness
softness	soft + ness
tenderness	tender + ness

....

➤ NOTE

....

1. **When –full is joined as a suffix it loses one '1'.**
   careful
   forgetful
   painful
2. **When –fully is joined as a suffix it keeps both '1's.**
   carefully
   forgetfully
   peacefully

....

11. *Final single consonant + suffix* starting with a vowel*

Rule: *Words that end with a single consonant double it before a suffix beginning with a vowel.*

get	getting
forget	forgetting
prefer	preferring
refer	referring
transfer	transferred
travel	travelled

*For prefix and suffix see Glossary of Grammatical Terms pp. 45–50.

Six spelling traps with silent letters

Learn the groups of words with silent letters

Silent b

bomb	doubt	numb
climb	dumb	plumbing
comb	lamb	thumb
debt	limb	tomb

Silent g

consign	gnarled	neigh
design	gnash	resign
feign	gnat	sign
foreign	gnaw	sleigh

silent gh

borough	fright	thigh
bough	might	thorough
bought	nought	though
dough	plough	thought
fought	sight	through

Silent k

knack	knife	knock
knee	knight	knot
kneel	knit	know

Silent p

pneumatic	pseudonym	receipt
pneumonia	psychiatry	
psalm	psychology	

Silent w

wrangle	wreck	wrinkle
wrap	wrestle	wrist
wrath	wretch	write
wreath	wriggle	wrong
wrench	wring	wry

Pairs of Words that Confuse

accept
except
He *accepted* that he was responsible for his team and all *except* one found the way home.

affect
effect
The price was *affected* by its being a copy, but the actual *effect* was of the genuine article.

allowed
aloud
You are *allowed* to visit the church but not to speak *aloud*.

all ready
You should be *all ready* to leave by six o'clock tomorrow.

already
It is *already* six o'clock.

altar
alter
The painting above the church *altar* has been *altered* in the Victorian period.

bare **bear**	He looked at the *bare* landscape and felt he could not *bear* the isolation.
cease **seize**	She *ceased* to worry about the mistakes of the past, and *seized* the chance for the future.
coarse **course**	His language grew *coarse* in the *course* of the fierce argument.
council **counsel**	At the local *council* office, staff were available to *counsel* and advise the homeless.
continual **continuous**	The *continual* beating of the drum gave him a *continuous* headache which lasted all evening.
currant **current**	Muesli may contain grain, nuts and *currants* and is *currently* rising in popularity here.
desert **dessert**	The *Desert* Sands restaurant serves the most delicious sorbet for *dessert*.
die **dye**	It had been traditional, when someone *dies*, for mourners to dress in cloth *dyed* black.
draft **draught**	The first *draft* of the plan for the house did not include *draught*-proofing.
duel **dual**	The two drivers fought a *duel*, each to overtake the other on the *dual* carriageway.
elder **older**	He is my *elder* brother and is more than five years *older* than I am.

elicit **illicit**	She managed to *elicit* the confession from him that he was dealing in *illicit* drugs.
emigrant **immigrant**	People *emigrating* to a new country have to go through *immigration* before they are accepted.
flaunt **flout**	Some teenagers *flaunt* new fashions in order to *flout* authority.
formal **former**	The *formal* speech at prize-giving was much more interesting than that given at the *former* event.
hear **here**	We went to *hear* the concert in Hyde Park by the Italian tenor who came *here* for the occasion.
hole **whole**	The *hole* in the centre of the sculpture was a significant part of the *whole* effect.
industrial **industrious**	On the *industrial* estate the workers were very *industrious* in expanding production rates.
in to **into**	They went *in to* face the angry principal, who led them *into* her study.
it's **its**	*It's* a miracle that *its* wrapping did not come loose in the post.
later **latter**	Come along *later*, after the nine o'clock interval, and enjoy the *latter* half of the concert.
lead **led**	The value of *lead* as a roofing material has *led* to some thefts from old buildings.

leant **lent**	As a student he *leant* on his parents to help him pay his way; they *lent* him money for a while.
loose **lose**	If your hub cap is *loose* you run the risk of *losing* it on the road.
luxuriant **luxurious**	The plant was of *luxuriant* growth and stood in a valuable and *luxurious* ceramic pot.
knew **new**	They *knew* the song from the 1960s, but this recording was by a *new* young singer.
peace **piece**	If you want world *peace* you should start with *piece by piece* negotiations.
personal **personnel**	The *personal* records of the company staff were kept in the *personnel* officer's care.
practical **practicable**	Martin is very *practical*; he's just patented a fold-up exercise machine – a *practicable* design.
practice **practise**	If you do your music *practice* regularly, and *practise* the set piece, you may win the prize.
principal **principle**	The *principal* of the college was liked and trusted by all for his moral *principles*.
precede **proceed**	Taking GCSE *precedes* taking A-Level examinations; if you pass the first you may *proceed* to the second.

prophecy **prophesy**	It's a *prophecy* likely to be fulfilled if you *prophesy* that a national lottery will be popular.
quiet **quite**	Keeping young children *quiet* is *quite* easy if you take care to keep them interested.
re-cover **recover**	She *re-covered* the roots of the plant with soil, so that it would *recover* from drought.
re-sign **resign**	The manager expected employees to *re-sign* and accept new contracts, or *resign* their jobs.
right **write**	You are doing the essay the *right* way, but you need to *write* it more legibly.
seasonable **seasonal**	We are cheered by *seasonable* cards and gifts at Christmas, despite *seasonal* cold weather.
sew **sow**	The star pupil used to *sew* beautifully, but that *sowed* seeds of envy in the rest of us.
sight **site**	The *sightseers* looked eagerly over the ancient *site* of the Temple of Thebes.
sole **soul**	The niece was the *sole* beneficiary of the will as she was the only living *soul* related to him.
stationary **stationery**	She left her car *stationary* on a yellow line while she went to buy *stationery* for letters.
their **there**	*Their* coats are in the cloakroom, just over *there* by the door.

threw **through**	He went white with shock when he *threw* the ball accidentally *through* the pavilion window.
to **too**	Don't try *to* help him by spending *too* much of your time and spoiling your own chances.
waist **waste**	She lost so much weight that, although her *waist-line* improved, she almost *wasted* away.
weather **whether**	The newspaper seller was out in all *weathers*, *whether* it was hot or cold, wet or dry.
were **we're**	We *were* going to travel on to France, but *we're* running out of money.
who's **whose**	*Who's* the owner of the red Jaguar outside? It's a car *whose* owner must be proud of it.
your **you're**	*Your* confidence may suffer at first when *you're* a new young employee at work.

Words Commonly Misspelt

A

absence	acquaintance	apostrophe
accelerate	acquire	apparent
accept	address	appearance
accident	adjacent	approximate
accommodation	admission	argument
accompany	advice	attachment
accomplish	affect	attendance

according
account
accumulate
accurate
accuse
achieve
acknowledge

allotted
allowance
although
altogether
anniversary
announcement
annual

attitude
audible
audience
authority
autumn
awe
awful

B

bachelor
barrel
barrier
basis
batch
beauty

beautiful
because
beginning
behaviour
beliefs
bicycle

bomb
borough
bought
brought
burglar
business

C

calendar
calves
cancelled
careful
carriage
catch
caught
ceiling
channel

clearance
climb
coarse
collision
colonel
colour
commence
commitment
committee

conductor
conquered
conscience
consequence
consign
contemptible
continual
convenience
correspondent

chauffeur complement cough
chief compliment council
choir concede currant
chord conceit current

D

daughter descent disappoint
debt description disastrous
deceit desert discipline
deceive design dismiss
defence despatch disobedient
deferred detachment dissatisfied
defiance develop divisible
deficient device doubt
dependant difference draught
dependence disagreeable dyeing

E

earliest eight error
easiest embarrass exaggerate
eccentric emigrant exceed
echoes emphasis excellence
edible endeavour exceptional
effect enough excess
efficient environment extravagant

F

familiar
fatal
fault
favour
fetch
field
fierce

flavour
forcible
foreign
foretell
forgetful
forgotten
formally

formerly
fought
fraud
frequent
friend
fulfilment
fulfilled

G

gaiety
gallop
gases
gauge
geography
ghastly

ghetto
glamorous
gnarled
governor
gradient
gradual

grammar
grief
grievance
guarantee
guard
gulf

H

halves
happening
happily
harassed
heavier

height
helpful
helpfully
hoard
honorary

honour
hoping
horrible
humorous
humour

I

ignorance	indebted	insure
illness	indelible	intelligence
immediate	infallible	intercede
immense	innocence	interference
important	innumerable	interrupt
impossible	insolence	irregular
incense	instructor	irritable
inconvenient	insurance	issue

J

jewellery	judgement (or judgment)	junior

K

keenness	knelt	knives
kitchen	knew	knock
knack	knife	knot
knee	knight	knowledge
kneed	knit	known

L

label	legible	lightening
labelled	leisure	lightning
labour	levelled	limb
language	licence	loose
laugh	license	lose
leant	lieutenant	luggage

M

machinery
magnificent
manual
marriage
match
medal
meddle

memories
memory
message
messenger
might
miseries
misery

misspelt
model
monarch
motor
mottoes
moustache
muscle

N

naughty
necessity
necessarily
negligent

neighbour
nephew
niece
notch

noticeable
nought
nuisance
numb

O

obedience
occasion
occasional
occupied
occupy
occur

occurred
odorous
odour
omission
omit
opponent

opportunity
opposite
oppress
orchestra
orphan
override

P

paragraph
parallel
parent
particular
passage
passenger
patch
patience
pause
peaceable
peaceful
peculiar
people
perceive
permission
permitted

perseverance
personal
personnel
persuade
phase
phrase
physique
plainness
plateau
pleasant
plentiful
plumb
pneumonia
possible
practice
practise

precede
preference
preferred
presence
pressure
principal
principle
procession
profession
proficient
prophecy
prophesy
provision
psalm
psychology
pursuit

Q

quaint
quality
quantity

quarrelled
quarter
quay

quench
quiet
quite

R

razor
recede
receipt

referred
reign
reliance

restaurant
retrieved
roofs

receive
recommend
reference

reluctant
resemblance
rumour

rough
ruinous
running

S

sadder
sandwich
sauce
scarves
scattered
schedule
scheme
science
scissors
seize
senior
sentence
sergeant

session
settlement
siege
sieve
sign
signal
silence
similar
skies
skilful
skilfully
sleigh
solicitor

sphere
squabble
square
stationary
stationery
stopping
stretch
submission
succeed
sufficient
support
survivor
symphony

T

tactful
tactfully
tailor
taught
tennis
terrible
terror
thatched
thief

thorough
though
thought
through
thumb
till
tobacco
tomb
tough

transmission
travel
travelled
treacherous
triumph
trough
truly
truthfully
tyranny

U

umbrella
unanimous
unassuming

unconscious
unforgettable
unique

unnecessary
until
utmost

V

valorous
valour
variety
vehicle

vein
vengeance
vigorous
vigour

villain
violence
visible
visitor

W

waist
waste
watch
weather
weigh
weight
weird
welcome
wharves

whether
whole
wholly
wilfully
withhold
women
woollen
woolly
wrap

wrench
wreck
wrestle
wretch
wring
wrist
writing
written
wrong

X

xenophobia

xerox

xylophone

Y

yacht   yawn   yield

Z

zeal   zinc   zoology

Spelling Routine
Ideas to Improve your Spelling

- Pick out words to learn from your own writing.
- Record them in a notebook or spelling file.
- Decide which method (see below) to use as a learning strategy.
- Practise them weekly until you know them.
- Use them in your writing. Do not just make lists of words.
- Find out about similar words e.g. with the same prefix or suffix.
- Get to know some spelling rules (described above) and match errors to the rules.
- Learn to build long words from root stems.
- When reading, if you come across a new word, look it up and learn the spelling.

Ways to Learn Spellings

As you know, English has 40 sounds and only 26 letters to express them by. That is why many letters have more than one sound:

cut/**k**it;   **g**entleman/**g**irl;   b**u**t/p**u**t

and often the same groups of letters combine to make a different sound:

r**ough**/thr**ough**;   ch**ea**p/d**ea**r;   l**o**ng/l**o**t.

Ten Strategies for Remembering Spellings

- Remember the *shape* of the word, e.g. canal, damage, defend.
- Break the word down *into parts*, e.g. can–al, dam–age.
- Exaggerate the pronunciation, e.g. dama*ge*, can*al*, de*fend*.
- Spell it as it sounds, e.g. canal, defend.
- Match it to word families:

  defend
  pretend.

- Apply rules to it: –or suffixes for trades and professions
  –er suffixes for other words.

  defender
  pretender

  BUT   conductor
  director

- Break it down into root, prefix and/or suffix:

  defend–er

  pretend–er
- Find words within words:

  disestablishment

  establish

  disestablish
- Mnemonics (memory tricks)

  stationEry has an 'e' because

  you write lEttErs with it.
- Look, cover, write, check.

  Don't copy a word down but learn it by

  LOOKing it up in a dictionary

  COVERing the word up

  WRITING the word from memory

  CHECKing against the dictionary

Spelling Exercises
Which is It?

Here are some paired examples for you to try for yourself.

1. She brushed her *luxurious/luxuriant* hair before the mirror
   until it shone like a halo.
2. He waited at the café table wondering *whether/weather* she
   would join him there.
3. A combined washing and drying machine proved to be a
   practical/practicable idea from the viewpoint of the manu-
   facturers.

4. He visited the *industrious/industrial* site of the old steel works.
5. She put him on the spot and hoped to *illicit/elicit* a confession of guilt from him.
6. The *continuous/continual* striking of the clock began to irritate him.
7. As the path was narrow, they needed to *precede/proceed* with caution.
8. He went to school and learned to read and write so he became the only *literary/literate* member of his family.
9. The *principle/principal* ballerina had strained her foot, so her understudy took over.
10. She left her vehicle *stationery/stationary* on a double yellow line.
11. She tried to lose *wait/weight* before her summer holidays.
12. Going to ancient *sites/sights* is very thrilling for *siteseers/sightseers.*

Grammar

Glossary of Grammatical Terms

abbreviation shortened form of a word/s in writing. E.g. Dr., e.g., etc.

acronym word made up from first letters of name of association. E.g. UNO, FIFA, ERNIE.

active having for subject the person or thing doing the action. E.g. The boy *kicks* the ball.

adjective a word describing a noun. E.g. The *leather* ball.

adverb a word adding to the meaning of a verb. E.g. The ball soared *high*.

affix a group of letters added at the start or end of a word to change its meaning. E.g. *un*fair fair*ly*. (See also **prefix** and **suffix**.)

antonym a word opposite in meaning to another. E.g. *good* is the antonym of bad. (See also **synonym**.)

auxiliary verb that is attached to another verb. E.g. I *did* go.

capital letter written in large form (upper case). E.g. *F*.

casual informal style of speech or writing. E.g. *The Friday match has been scratched.*

clause a group of words forming a sentence or part of one, with a subject and a finite verb. E.g. *The star player kicked the ball* and *he scored a goal.*

collocation a group of words usually put together. E.g. *Fish and chips* rather than fish and onions.

command to order – imperative mood of the verb. E.g. *Get out!*   45

comparative increase in quality, quantity or degree of adjectives or adverbs. E.g. *louder* singing; to sing *more loudly*.

complex a sentence with several clauses. E.g. *Although he loved cricket, and always practised hard at it, he was very keen on tennis as well.*

compound a sentence consisting of two main parts. E.g. *He loved cricket and always practised hard.*

conditional verb following 'if' or 'unless'. E.g. If I *were* you I'd try harder.

conjunction words connecting two parts of a compound sentence. E.g. *and, but, so, yet, or, nor.*

consonant any letter of the alphabet except for *a,e,i,o,u; y* is sometimes a consonant (e.g. *yesterday*); sometimes a vowel (e.g. *worrying*).

consultative style of speech or writing between people who are acquainted, but not very closely so. E.g. *Did you know that Friday's match may be cancelled?*

continuous ongoing action. E.g. He *was running* fast.

contraction shortened form of a word/s. E.g. cannot = *can't*.

co-ordination two clauses equal in grammatical importance. E.g. *He could swim and he could dive, too.*

definite article the word 'the'. (See also **indefinite article**.)

determiner a word limiting the meaning of a noun and preceding adjectives. E.g. This *cricket* ball.

dipthong a combined vowel made by blending two vowels. E.g. *mediaeval*

exclamation mark a mark written after words expressing a strong feeling or sentiment. E.g. *You're out!*

finite verb 'am', 'was', 'are' are finite forms of the verb. (See also **non-finite**.)

formal tone rule-bound 'correct' style. E.g. *It is possible that the match may not take place on Friday.*

formula (in speech) set of words repeated usually for the sake of politeness. E.g. *How are you? I'm fine.*

formula (in writing) set pattern of writing fiction. E.g. fairy story, romance, western.

frozen style icily formal speech or writing. E.g. *It is understood that the soccer fixture may have to be cancelled on Friday.* (See also **casual**, **consultative**, **formal tone** and **intimate style**.)

idiom a phrase conveying something other than the literal meaning. E.g. *it's not cricket!*

imperative (See **command**.)

imperfect tense tense of the verb showing an incomplete action. E.g. He *was running* hard …

indefinite article the words 'a' or 'an'.

infinitive form of the verb preceded by 'to' and used after other verbs. E.g. I want *to see* the match.

interjection a word or phrase used in a sudden remark. E.g. Well, *no*, I didn't catch it.

interrogative (See **question**.)

intimate style very relaxed discourse, usually between two. E.g. *Friday's match is off.*

intransitive a verb which has a subject but no object. E.g. He *paused*. (See **transitive**.)

major sentence sentence with a subject and a verb. E.g. *The ball was lost.*

minor sentence sentence which is grammatically incomplete but correct for the context. E.g. *Not out!*

non-finite verb 'being' and 'been' are non' finite forms of the verb. (See **finite**.)

noun a word that is the name of a person, place or thing, quality or action and is used as the subject or object of a verb or preposition. E.g. The *boy* threw the *ball*. The *ball* hit the *net*.

participle past part of the verb, may also be used as an adjective. E.g. It was *lost*. A *lost* ball.

participle present part of the verb, may also be used as an adjective. E.g. He is *running*. A *running* man.

passive voice expressing an action done to the subject. E.g. The ball *was hit* by the player.

perfect tense past tense of verb showing a period of time in the past. E.g. *I had played* in past years.

perfect tense present tense of verb showing a period of time up to the present. E.g. I *have played* this week.

perfect tense future tense of verb showing a period of time in the future. E.g. I *will have played* again.

phonetic system of writing down spoken sounds of an individual speaker.

phrasal verb a group of words including an adverb or preposition with a verbal function. E.g. *bowled out.*

phrase a group of words lacking a finite verb. E.g. *Coming up for half-time*; *a good wicket.*

plural form of a word expressing more than one thing. E.g. *pavilions*; *umpires*; *sweaters.*

possessive form of a word showing possession or ownership. E.g. *his, her, mine, Jane's.*

pre-determiner word that precedes 'a' or 'the'. E.g. *Such* a good hit; *all* the runs.

prefix an affix placed at the beginning of a word. E.g. *pre*-arranged. (See **affix** and **suffix**.)

preposition a word added to a noun to form a phrase. E.g. *at* home.

pronoun a word replacing a noun or noun phrase. E.g. *He* arrived.

question sentence or phrase asking for information. E.g. *Is it over yet?*

reflexive verb the action of the verb affects the person performing the action. E.g. I hurt *myself.*

simple a sentence with only one main verb. E.g. *The spectators applauded.*

singular a word or grammatical form representing one. E.g. *field, run.* (See **plural**)

split infinitive to place a word dividing the infinitive. E.g. *to wildly hit.*

statement a written or spoken declaration. E.g. *I love sport*

subordinate joined to a sentence but cannot stand alone. E.g. *While I was watching the game,* I cheered.

suffix an affix placed at the end of a word. E.g. excite*ment*. (See affix and prefix.)

superlative greatest degree of comparison of an adjective or adverb. E.g. the *hardest* hit; to sing *most* beautifully.

syllable a word or part of a word containing a vowel. E.g. *dis–put–ed; un–fair.*

synonym a word with a very similar meaning to another word in the same language. E.g. *bad, evil.*

tag a phrase added to the end of a statement to make it a question. E.g. It's out, *isn't it?*

tense a form of the verb showing time, continuing or completion of an action. E.g. I *go* (present) I *went* (past); I *will* go (future).

transitive a verb which takes a direct object. E.g. She *kept* the score.

verb a word or phrase telling of action or experience. E.g. They *won*.

voice the form of the verb showing whether the subject acts or is acted upon. E.g. They *won*. It *was won*. (See **active** and **passive voice**.)

vowel letters 'a' 'e' 'i' 'o' 'u' and 'y'. (See **consonants**.)

Common Grammatical Errors

A

a or an?

Rule: *Use **an** before a vowel:*
It was *an* uncomfortable bed.

*Use **an** before a silent h:*
She waited *an* hour for a bus.

*Otherwise, use **a**:*
There was *a* crowd at the gates.

affect or effect?

Rule: *Use **affect** to mean influence; use **effect** to mean bring about.*

The audience was *affected* emotionally by the film, with the *effect* that it was a huge box office success.

all ready or already?

Rule: *Use **all ready** to mean everyone/thing is prepared; use **already** to mean so soon.*
The Wimbledon crowd fell silent, *all ready* for the final set of the match, and the two players were *already* on court.

all right or alright?

Rule: *Write **all right** to mean safe, healthy, satisfactory, in order.* (The misspelling alright is a common error.)
It is *all right* to walk into the road with traffic approaching so long as you are on a zebra crossing.

all together or altogether?

Rule: *Use **all together** to mean people or things in a group; use **altogether** to mean entirely.*
We huddled *all together* under an awning when it began to rain *altogether* unexpectedly.

amount or number?

Rule: *An **amount** refers to a mass of things; **number** refers to a countable group.*
The total fund exceeded the *amount* that the Scouts had hoped to collect because a large *number* of them had joined in the fund raising.

anybody and **anyone**

Rule: *These are singular.*
Anybody is permitted to visit the law courts.

B

but or **and**?

Rule: *Use **but** for contrastive clauses and phrases; use **and** for comparative clauses and phrases.*
She wanted to pay *but* her friend advised against it.
She wanted to pay *and* her friend agreed with her.

C

compared to or **compared with**?

Rule: *Use **compared to** when you judge one thing against another; use **compared with** when you judge a smaller, lesser thing against a bigger, greater one.*
London opera is underfunded *compared to* that of Paris.
London opera is well funded *compared with* provincial music.

D

different from or **different to**?

Rule: *Use **different from** in writing; **different to** is often used in speech nowadays.*
The whole experience of the cruise was *different from* our expectation of it.

E

each

Rule: ***Each*** *is singular.*
Each student should check *his/her* result carefully.

each other or one another?

Rule: *Use **each other** when referring to two people or things; use **one another** when referring to more than two.*
The two friends usually competed against *each other*, but in the class project they decided to join a group and support *one another.*

either ... or?

Rule: *each one of the pair begins a new phrase or clause.*
We *either* fight *or* we go under.

every, everybody, everyone

Rule: *These are singular.*
Every doctor keeps information about *his/her* patients confidential so that *everybody* is able to talk to the doctor openly about *his or her* health.

F

farther or further?

Rule: *Use **farther** for distance but **further** for quantity.*
The people travelled *farther* than they had expected and then found that there was still a *further* two miles to go.

few or less?

Rule: *Use **few** to refer to countable numbers, use **less** to refer to amount.*
There was *less* fabric than I had ordered and *fewer* customers requested it, luckily.

former

Rule: *Use **former** only to refer to one of two persons or things.*
Given an opportunity to visit either Florence or Rome, she chose the *former*.

H

hardly

Rule: ***Hardly** has a negative sense and does not go with no, not.*
He had *hardly* enough money for his fare.

he or him?

Rule: ***He** is the subject; **him** is the object of the sentence.*
He wrote to his cousin and asked *him* to come to see *him*.

hers or her's?

Rule: *The possessive pronoun has no apostrophe.*
When asked about the lost bag, she said it was *hers*.

I

I or **me**?

Rule: *I is the subject;* ***me*** *is the object in the sentence.*
I am cleared of the crime as my barrister defended *me* well.

its or **it's**?

Rule: *The possessive adjective or pronoun has no apostrophe.*
Its bodywork was rusty so the car failed *its* MOT.

Rule: *The contraction* ***it's*** = *it is and has an apostrophe.*
It's clear that *it's* going to rain today.

L

latter, later or last?

Rule: *Use* ***latter*** *to refer to one of two persons or things in order; use* ***later*** *to refer to one or two persons or things in a time sequence; use* ***last*** *to refer to one of a group.*
In the *latter* part of the holiday it snowed, even though Easter was *later* than usual. That was the *last* type of weather we had expected.

to lay or to lie?

Rule: *The verb* ***to lay*** *takes an object but to lie does not.*
I *lay* my head on a pillow as I *lie* resting.

55

M

majority or most?

Rule: *Use **majority** for countable numbers; otherwise use **most**.*
The *majority* of MPs have work other than their duties in Parliament; *most* of their income comes from outside sources.

myself or I?

Rule: ***Myself** (reflexive) is used when the action of the verb affects the person doing the action. Do not use it as an alternative to **I**.*
I believed in *myself*, first and foremost.

N

neither or none?

Rule: *Use **neither** to refer to one of two persons or things; use **none** to refer to more than two persons or things.*
Neither of my two brothers liked sport and I was bad at it, too, so my father was disappointed that *none* of his children would follow his example and play for England.

nobody, no one?

Rule: *These are singular.*
Nobody likes to be misunderstood. There is *no one* in the world you know better than yourself.

number of?

Rule: *This phrase takes a plural verb.*
A large *number of* tourists *are* crowding into town.

no/not?

Rule: *Two negatives make a positive.*
I did *not* have *nothing* to declare at the airport =
I had something to declare.

O

one ... one/one ... you?

Rule: *Keep to the same pronoun consistently in a sentence.*
One should take care to carry *one's* film in *one's* hand luggage
when *one* is travelling by air.

ones or one's

Rule: *Use **ones** to refer to several persons or things; use **one's** to show possession.*
Looking at the apples on the stall I chose the green *ones*
because I had been told that they are good for *one's* teeth.

P

passed or past?

Rule: *Use **passed** for the past participle or tense; **past** as an adjective.*
The years had *passed* and now many of the things they had
enjoyed most were *past* memories.

practice or practise?

Rule: *Use **practice** for the noun, **practise** for the verb.*
He managed to improve his fingering by constantly *practising*
on the guitar – as they say, '*practice* makes perfect'! 57

Q

quote or quotation?

Rule: *Use **quote** for the verb, **quotation** for the noun.*
I asked for a *quotation* for the cost of repair, and he *quoted* me a very reasonable sum.

R

round or around?

Rule: *Use **round** to mean by way or, near, and **around** to mean on all sides.*
People gathered *around* the astronomical clock *round* about noon to see the best display of action.

S

scarcely

Rule: ***Scarcely** has a negative sense, and does not go with no, not.*
There were *scarcely* any plants in flower for the show because of the cold weather.
(See also **hardly**.)

she or her?

Rule: ***She** is a personal pronoun as subject; **her** is a possessive adjective, or pronoun as object.*
She always tried *her* best to please *her* parents who repaid *her* with their love.

somebody or someone?

Rule: *These are singular.*
Somebody needs to take charge here.

subject and verb – singular or plural?

Rule: *The verb agrees with the subject, not the closest noun.*
The *bag* of apples *has* broken open.

T

their, there or they're?

Rule: *Use **their** to show possession; use **there** to show direction, place, position; use **they're** as a contraction of they are.*
They're sure that *their* sports bags were left over *there* on the lockers.

there is or there are?

Rule: *The verb matches the object.*
It is clear that *there are more details* about the post than *there is space* to include them.

W

we or us?

Rule: ***We** is the subject and **us** is the object in a sentence.*
We two parents and you, our daughter, have to pay extra to travel first class; they have *given us* better seats.

were or **was?**

Rule: *After if (conditional clause) use **were** not **was**.*
If I were you I would go early to make sure of a place.

who or **whom?**

Rule: *Use **who** as the subject of the verb, otherwise use **whom**.*
The man *who* called here yesterday is the applicant to whom I promised employment.

➤ **NOTE**

In speech and casual writing this rule is often broken.

Basic Grammatical Structures
The Phrase

The Phrase does not have both a noun subject and a verb. It may have just a noun, just a verb or neither.

Noun Phrases

       the team captain

       the rosewood box

Verb Phrases

       sitting comfortably

       had been bought

Prepositional Phrases

> in the club house

> at an antique shop

Sentences

Sentences have both a noun as subject and a verb as predicate.

Simple Sentences These have only one subject and one predicate.

> I lost my wallet.

> Rain set in early.

Compound Sentences These have at least two main nouns and verbs.

> I lost my wallet and I was very upset about it.

> Rain set in early but it cleared up after lunch.

Complex Sentences These have one main noun and verb and a subordinate noun and verb.

> I lost my wallet when I was hurrying to the shops.

> Because rain set in early, the match was postponed.

Four Main Types of Sentence The four main types of sentence are:

1. *Statements*

> She refused the offer.

2. *Orders*

> Refuse the offer.

3. *Questions*

> Did she refuse the offer?

➤ **NOTE**

Tag questions are statements, with an additional question at the end.

> E.g. She refused the offer, didn't she?

---

4. *Exclamations*

> She actually refused the offer!

Minor Sentences Sentences without a main noun and verb are sentence fragments or minor sentences. You should usually avoid them in your work. However, there are some kinds of writing where they are appropriate.

Direct Speech

To make this sound natural, you will need to use some minor sentences.

> Sally rushed in, banging the classroom door. "Is Mrs. Rushton in this morning?" she asked. "*Not yet,*" her friend replied, reassuringly.

> The two sat locked in tension when the car stopped at the lights. He broke the silence by saying, "*What about last night?*" "*What about it?*" she snapped.

Dialogue

Most stage plays have speech containing minor sentences.

> The attendant: Stop! No entry!

> Visitor: Why?

(Imagine how stiff and unnatural it would sound in major sentence.)

> The attendant: I am asking you, Sir, if you will please respect the notice and not enter there.

> Visitor: Why are you making this request?

Greetings

We use a great many minor sentences every day to 'break the ice' when meeting people we know slightly but with whom we do not want to get into extended conversation. These brief remarks are known as 'formula' greetings.

> "How are you?" "Fine!"

> "Have a nice day." "You, too."

Maxims and Proverbs

Some of these old phrases have become worn away through time, so that only the essential words remain. These are minor sentences because they are complete in themselves, so far as their meaning is concerned.

> Easy come, easy go. Least said, soonest mended.

Telegraphic Writing

This is writing where there is not time or space for full major sentences but the minor sentence is fully understood and so complete.

Notices: NO ENTRY   VACANCIES   FIRE NOTICE   NO PARKING

Titles: <u>J.F.K</u>   <u>Reservoir Dogs</u>   <u>Gone with the Wind</u>
<u>Jaws</u>   <u>Wuthering Heights</u>   <u>The Color Purple</u>
<u>Cry, Freedom!</u>   <u>Moonlight Sonata</u>
<u>Bohemian Rhapsody</u>   <u>Help!</u>

Headlines: PEACE PACT MISSION   MINISTER QUITS
STAR MAKES COMEBACK

Beware of the double meaning that leaving out parts of the
sentence can cause.

GIANT WAVES DOWN TUNNEL

GENERAL FLIES BACK TO FRONT

QUEEN QUITS

Sentence Exercise

Which of these *song titles* are major sentences (i.e. have a main
noun and a main verb)?
1. Singing in the Rain
2. I'm not in Love
3. All you need is Love
4. I only have Eyes for You
5. You make me feel so Young

6. When a Man loves a Woman
7. I will survive
8. Go, now
9. It's got to be perfect
10. Where have all the Flowers gone?

Which of these *book titles* are minor sentences?

1. The Heart of the Matter
2. One Flew over the Cuckoo's Nest
3. A Room with a View
4. War and Peace
5. The Spy who came in from the Cold
6. Swiss Family Robinson
7. Life, a User's Manual
8. Dead Men don't Talk
9. Life is a Beach
10. Born Free

Now, can you identify the major and the minor titles from the following list of *film titles?*

1. The Postman always rings Twice
2. Love Story
3. Hell is for Heroes
4. Guess who's coming to Dinner?
5. After Office Hours
6. All about Eve
7. The Good, the Bad and the Ugly

8. Around the World in Eighty Days
9. Birth of a Nation
10. Gentlemen Prefer Blondes

And can you identify the major and minor sentences from the following list of *radio and television programmes?*

1. If you are so Clever, why aren't you Rich?
2. Any Questions?
3. Not the Nine o'Clock News
4. The London Programme
5. Crime Watch
6. The Antiques Road Show
7. Are you Being Served?
8. That was the week that was
9. Desert Island Discs
10. The Day that Changed my Life

Effective Sentences

Here are some ways of writing effective sentences in composition.

Antithesis

Here the two halves of the sentence contrast.

> Why should I dress up? When I am at home, everyone recognizes me and when I am in town, nobody recognizes me.

Balanced sentence

Here the two halves of the sentence have the same grammatical structure.

> Love is positive; love is patient.

Ladder sentence

Emphasis is gained by building up phrases and clauses in ascending order, until a climax is reached.

> City life is environmentally unhealthy, chronically dangerous and morally corrupting.

Metaphor

Here you compare two dissimilar things, without using 'like' or 'as'.

> Home once was the girl's prison and the woman's workhouse.

Paradox

This is a statement that seems contradictory but may well be true.

> Love and need are one.

Parallelism

This is building up sentences with similar (grammatically equal) structures.

> She had no time to be happy, no time to be human.

Repetition

Here you repeat ideas or phrases for extra emphasis.

> He worked hard at his job and worked hard on his house. He even worked hard at his marriage.

Rhetorical question

A question which is left for the reader to answer is often a good way of attracting attention. Do not over do this effect, though, or it may seem mannered.

> What have you done in your lifetime to help the disadvantaged? Have you done anything?

Short sentence

A short sentence can have sudden, dramatic effect.

> In the closing years of a century it is tempting to look ahead and think what the future may bring. We may wonder, but only our children and our grandchildren will be sure of it. No one can tell.

Simile

This is a comparison, introduced by 'like' or 'as'.

> My love is like a red, red rose.

> She felt as free as a bird.

Skills

Homework Tips
1. *Establish good habits of study*

Study is easier if done regularly, so here are some tips to help you to make the best use of your homework time.

- Find a time when you are free to study and keep to it.
- If you miss a study session, make it up. Don't postpone your work and get behind.
- Decide where you will work and keep to it.
- Make a grand plan of your study schedule, counting down from the examination/test day, week by week until it is full.
- Be businesslike in your record-keeping: have a working folder or disk, and date it each time you add to it.
- Include all draft work in your folder – do not throw it away or work on scraps of paper.
- Complete work as you go. If you have a back-log of unfinished work it will worry you and so make it hard to proceed.
- Be disciplined about spending your scheduled time studying – not half of it making coffee and phone calls to friends.
- Review what you have achieved each week. Make a note of where you intend to start next session.
- Allow some time for the unexpected. You may be able to have a second try at a piece of work that was on the wrong lines.

2. *Brush up on your literacy skills*

- Consider improving your reading strategies. Do you read too slowly, or everything at the same speed? Find out about speed-reading for processing material quickly.
- Learn to :

    skim: glance over a page quickly to get the main idea;

    scan: read steadily to pick up general details;

    search read: read carefully with scrutiny to find exact information;

    SQ3R: skim and scan/ask a question/read steadily/recall what you have read/review the text to check your understanding and retention of it.

THIS IS A GOOD TECHNIQUE FOR EXAM REVISION!

- Consider reading for different levels of meaning:

    reading the lines: literal comprehension i.e. understanding the words on the page;

    reading between the lines: inferential comprehension i.e. understand part of the meaning and work out the rest;

    reading beyond the lines: symbolic comprehension i.e. using experience of life to understand text.

- Improve your note-taking

    be *selective and businesslike;* only note what you need to know;

    try a *colour-coding system:* main ideas in red, subsidiary ideas in blue, examples in green and quotations in black;

consider using a *card-index system:* with less space you
have to be selective, and then you can rearrange
notes in a flexible way;

keep a *data-base* on disk and reorganize it, update it regularly.

3. *Learn how to plan your work*

- Find out about brainstorming i.e. sharing ideas in a group:

  flow-charts/mind maps i.e. flexible sketch planning;

  topic trees i.e. refining and structuring work;

  formal outlines i.e. writing up in correct form your planning ideas.

- Learn different structures to suit your needs e.g:

  chronological: by date sequence;

  criteria: by main characteristics;

  causal: reasons for and causes;

  compare/contrast: like with like, like against different;

  dynamic: strongest ideas first.

- Practise improving your work by drafting, discussing the
  draft and making a fair, corrected, well-presented final copy.

4. *Make good use of local resources*

- Visit your local library reference section and get to know
  relevant sources of information there.

- Book time on the computers available there.

- Make a card index of books, journals, videos, CD-Roms that will be useful to you in your work.
- Talk to the librarian when you need advice.

Coursework Tips
1. *Make use of the media*

- Find out from radio, TV and the computer information systems anything that will help you in your work.
- While you are watching TV be aware of the purpose and form of programmes and how they have been put across effectively.
- Try out, in your own work, attractive effects of style.
- Watch TV discussions and interviews and notice how people behave, especially in structuring their speeches, paying attention to the audience, and in their non-verbal communications (NVC).

2. *Gather source material more widely*

- Arrange to visit places of interest relevant to your course of study.
- Write to any companies or organizations relevant to your work.

3. *Extend your range of talking skills*

- Take every opportunity to discuss your ideas in small and large groups.

- Talk is a two-way communication process – learn to be a responsive listener.
- Watch other speakers' NVC – eye contact, gesture, posture.
- If you have the opportunity, try to talk to a large audience e.g. assembly.
- If there is one locally, join a debating or dramatic society – or, why not start one yourself!

4. *Extend your range of reading skills*

- Practise reading at different speeds for different purposes i.e. skimming, scanning and search reading.
- Try to find time to read beyond your school books e.g. newspapers, magazines, fiction, poetry.
- When you read, guess ahead, predict how the text will develop.
- Notice the way authors structure their work for your own use as a writer.
- Don't ignore words you don't understand. Look them up in a dictionary.
- Keep a glossary (simple word list with explanations) of new words and concepts.
- Occasionally, reread a text and be aware that you notice different things each time you read.

5. *Extend your range of writing skills*

- Don't keep to a narrow range e.g. personal writing. Branch out to try narrative, descriptive, dramatic, persuasive, poetic writing, especially for your coursework folder.

- Practise functional writing – summarizing, reporting.
- Practise critical writing – evaluating, comparing, contrasting, reviewing.
- Try writing about the same content from two different points of view e.g. hero and victim.
- Try writing about the same content in two different forms e.g. monologue and police report.
- Try writing about the same content in two different styles e.g. frozen/formal – headteacher; casual – nervous pupil.

6. *Learn to evolve work through drafting and editing*

- Keep a writer's notebook and jot down good ideas for writing.
- Practise editing, cutting and pasting to shape your work.
- Practise proof-reading to correct and refine your work.
- Take care with spelling, handwriting and good presentation for the final version.

Examination Tips
Terminal Examination

- Go to bed early. Try to relax and don't revise late.
- Have a good breakfast and set off early so that you won't panic if you are delayed on the journey.
- Remember that it is natural to be nervous!
- When you get the paper, read all the instructions carefully once or twice.

- Mark out in pencil what you intend to answer, and check then that you have noticed all the parts of questions required.
- Notice which questions have most marks. Do those first.
- Notice key words in questions (see list below) and see that you fulfil their requirements.
- Check if there are any word limits. If so, keep to them.
- Make sure that you keep to the point. Check for relevance.
- If you make mistakes – cross out boldly what is wrong and rewrite it.
- Time your answers so that you will finish the paper.
- Try to leave time to look over your paper as 'editor' to pick up any careless errors.
- Check that you have crossed through all rough work, drafts, and false starts that you don't want the examiner to mark.
- If you have written continuation parts (afterthoughts) make sure that they are clearly labelled with the number of the question they relate to.
- Check that the numbers of questions are listed on the front cover in the order you have tackled them, and also written above the relevant answers inside the booklet.
- Before handing in your paper, check that your examination number, centre number and name are correctly written on the front of the answer book.
- Finally, make sure that any extra sheets you have used are firmly tied to your answer book.
- *Then* you can hand the paper in, feeling that you have done your best!

Coursework Folders: Checking

- Make sure you know what the syllabus expects of you.
- Include the appropriate number of pieces of work.
- Include both Writing, and Speaking and Listening coursework.
- Include the appropriate range of pieces.
- Include some draft work to show how pieces evolved.
- Include some self-evaluation of the folder's contents.
- Check whether you have to include some handwritten pieces and how much work may be done on a computer.
- Include any teacher records of your work.
- Make sure that you have filled in the front page of the folder correctly, and signed the declaration that the contents are your own, unaided work.

Top Ten Tips for Revision

- Keep a balance between study, hobbies and social life.
- Keep your subjects interesting by relating them to the world outside, the media etc.
- Revise systematically. Draw up a plan early on and keep to it.
- Involve other people – friends and family. Discuss your working problems with them.
- Keep revision active i.e. make notes as you go, practise.
- Get to know exactly the examination requirements: find sample questions and practise those.
- Ask questions if you don't understand your work. Ask teachers, in the public library, through the Internet. Remember, questioning is active learning.

- Practise writing timed answers.
- Look forward. Remember there is life after exams! Plan to do something that is fun immediately afterwards.
- Look well ahead. Remember that all this effort is for your future – and it's worth it!

Words to Watch for in Examination Questions

Analyse: Break into separate parts and discuss, or interpret each part.

Compare: Examine two or more things, and pick out similarities.

Consider: Give opinions in relation to given information.

Contrast: Examine two or more things, and pick out differences.

Criticize: Make judgements; usually also give detail to support your views.

Debate: Consider both sides of the question and come to a conclusion.

Define: Give the meaning, or precise limits of the topic.

Describe: Give a detailed account of qualities, parts etc.

Discuss: Consider both sides of an issue; maybe compare and contrast, or focus on differences.

Enumerate: List several ideas, aspects, reasons, qualities.

Explain: Make an idea clear; show logical development with reasons.

Evaluate: Give your opinion or refer to those of critics. Include evidence, quotation, details in support.

Illustrate: Give major examples. Explain through examples, featuring them centrally.

Interpret: Explain the meaning of a text.

Outline: Give all the main ideas i.e. an overview of the subject.

Prove: Support fully with facts.

Relate: Show the connection between ideas and/or place them against broader relevant issues.

Review: Go back over earlier points briefly.

Sketch: Give main ideas briefly.

State: Explain precisely.

Summarize: Give a brief version, avoiding unnecessary details.

Trace: Show how events/arguments progress and develop.

Answers

Punctuation Exercises

A

On the 14th of June 1990, Ernest Threadfill, a 59 year-old accountant from Gloucester, thought to be involved in smuggling drugs, placed thirty one thousand pounds in a bag in a rubbish bin at Heathrow Airport, at one o'clock in the afternoon.

The bag was collected by Mr. Paul Frost, 25, with nine children, from 114 Furze Road, in South London, when he deposited what appeared to be a fast-food box, but which later was said to contain a number of packages of a substance thought to be heroin.

The British Broadcasting Corporation gave news coverage to this event at six o'clock in the afternoon, saying that both men had been detained for questioning.

Mr. Frost later was reported to have said that it was the hand of Fate. Newspapers carried headlines to the effect that two master criminals had been outwitted by the police.

B

It's the way he sits and waits, vaguely watching the television, vacantly staring out of the window – it haunts me, because he's just sitting and waiting. He forgets my name, my uncle's names, my cousins', but he always remembers Brutus, the dog. He seems to know who I am, but not why I'm here. I suppose I'm here to pass by some of that long, lonely waiting time with some light conversation. I'm here to prove that he has carried on his blood line. Maybe, I'm here to show it's all been worth it: four children, ten grandchildren, a fairly comfortable life; but does that bring any solace when now his life is spent just sitting, too weak to stand, waiting?

Spelling Exercises
Which is it?

1. luxuriant
2. whether
3. practicable
4. industrial
5. elicit
6. continual
7. proceed
8. literate
9. principal
10. stationary
11. weight
12. sites
    sightseers

Sentences Exercises

Song Titles: 2. 3. 4. 5. 7. 8. 9. 10.

Book Titles: 1. 3. 4. 5. 6. 7. 10.

Film Titles:

1. Major
2. Minor
3. Major
4. Major
5. Minor
6. Minor
7. Minor
8. Minor
9. Minor
10. Major

Programme Titles:

1. Major
2. Minor
3. Minor
4. Minor

5. Minor
6. Minor
7. Major
8. Major

9. Minor
10. Major